Morning Coffee with My Savior

How God Taught Me to Be Obedient
over Morning Coffee

Lisa Pearson

WESTBOW°
PRESS
A DIVISION OF THOMAS NELSON
& ZONDERVAN

Scripture taken from the New King James Version. Copyright 1979, 1980,
1982 by Thomas Nelson, inc. Used by permission. All rights reserved.

WestBow Press books may be ordered through
booksellers or by contacting:

WestBow Press
A Division of Thomas Nelson & Zondervan
1663 Liberty Drive
Bloomington, IN 47403
www.westbowpress.com
1 (866) 928-1240

Because of the dynamic nature of the Internet, any web addresses or
links contained in this book may have changed since publication and
may no longer be valid. The views expressed in this work are solely those
of the author and do not necessarily reflect the views of the publisher,
and the publisher hereby disclaims any responsibility for them.

Any people depicted in stock imagery provided by Thinkstock are models,
and such images are being used for illustrative purposes only.
Certain stock imagery © Thinkstock.

ISBN: 978-1-4908-9479-9 (sc)
ISBN: 978-1-4908-9480-5 (e)

Print information available on the last page.

WestBow Press rev. date: 03/03/2016

This book is dedicated to my beautiful Savior;
Because He loved me first

Table of Contents

Foreword

"Lisa Norred-Pearson has shared her own walk of faith in this inspiring and easy-read book. I could read through it all at one time or just little parts each day, like a devotional. She relates questions and parts from everyday life with passages from the Bible that just make sense. Christians need fellowship and motivational encouragement and this inspires both. Sometimes the feel is so warm; it's like having a chat with your sweet southern friend over coffee."

Laura Caine, Author of "Wildflowers" and the "Men of Highland" Series.

Acknowledgements

Tim and Madison, thank you for helping me grow daily; I love you more than you will ever know in this life. Tim you truly show me, to the best of your ability, how Christ loves the Church. You are my blessing from God. Madison, my precious gift from God, with you I get a glimpse of how much God loves us, and it humbles me to my knees.

My wonderful church family, Bro. Benny, you encourage us to go where we don't think we can and to stand firm when we don't think we will ever make it. Connie, thank you for holding me up, you wouldn't allow me to sink into the abyss of depression. Remember, God is using you when you don't even know it. I love you my beautiful and wonderful friend.

My brother and sister, I love you both bunches. Wendy, thank you letting me come to you with all of my garbage and unloading, and for not judging me. I am most blessed to get you as a sister, twice, by blood and through Christ. Jeff, keep your eyes on Jesus and write the songs He has for you. You are so talented, and I don't even think you know it.

Mom and Dad, what can I say, y'all are the best parents any child could hope for. Thank you both for leaving us children with something better than riches, a good name, a foundation built on Jesus and the most wonderful example of how God loves us unconditionally. Thank you for not compromising and showing us the true God!

Finally, Sherri Stanley-Miller, dear friend, I couldn't have done this without your brain! Thank you for the editing! Thank you for taking us all in your circle when you married Mr. Jerry! I love you both so much!

Introduction

My fellow warrior, where does your journey begin?

I think my journey started when I was in a bulldozer listening to the radio and I heard this wonderful Christian lady say something about tithing our time. Oh, how I wish I could remember her name. I would love to give her a hug and say "thank you," for helping get me started on the journey that I'm on today. She talked about if we tithe our money, shouldn't we also tithe our time? She said to just start with five minutes in the morning, and soon we would see it turn into fifteen minutes until we would not be able to do anything without spending time with our Savior. She said that if you say you don't have time to do that, try it, and see just how much more time your Lord gives you in that day. I'm a practical person and that just sounded practical. He provides all your financial needs (not wants) when you tithe, and wouldn't He also do that with your time? Needless to say, I probably started out with selfish reasons or to just try it out, but then it turned into the beginning of a Beautiful Friendship. Starting out your day with the Lord is so very important my fellow warriors, and why would we dare give the Creator of time, leftover time? When you are drinking your morning coffee, open the Word, talk to the Author, and see the beautiful journey that will start in your life. I bet it will be amazing!

Let me let you wonderful Christian people reading this in on a little something, if the Lord speaks to you through these words I am writing, and you tell Him no, you might as well put the book down now, until you are ready to give Him everything. I am an average person, no great talents, was **never** the best at anything. The **only** good thing in me is my Savior. That's it. So don't think to start your own journey or book or whatever you would like to call it, you have to be a Super Christian, nope, not at all. Read the story of Gideon. That's me. I ask God all the time, "Lord, what do You see in me? *How* can I possibly do the things you ask of me?" Do you ever find yourself asking that? Well, let me tell you the answer I got; He doesn't see my failures, my averageness, and my selfishness. He sees Himself in me, and as long as I keep telling Him "Yes", He will continue to work with me. It truly can be as simple as that my wonderful fellow warriors.

Chapter 1

Are Your Sacrifices Acceptable?

I didn't have any idea that I would be writing this, as a matter of fact, while writing it, I do still not quite believe I can do it. That's okay, as long as God leads me, I will give it my all.

This book got started when I was drinking my morning coffee and talking with my Savior about what I had just read in His word. I felt Him whisper in my heart to text what we were talking about to my fellow Christians and friends. I was terrified. You may ask yourself, "Why would she be scared to send a text to people she knows?" Well, I have a huge enemy out there that does not want me to encourage or help anyone have a closer walk with God. How does Satan attack me? He does it by putting fear in my heart. Praise to my Savior, He told me what was happening. I listened to the Voice that He promised me "I would know," and sent the text. You are now probably asking, "Oh my, what was this text about?" Well, I'm so glad you asked. I guess how important it is depends on your own walk, and where you are at in that walk. To some it may be elementary; to others it may change their life, as that beautiful lady on the radio changed mine.

The text was about the first chapter of Malachi. I will let you read that for yourselves, and I encourage you to do it. Don't take my word as truth, but take our Savior's Word as truth. In the first chapter of Malachi, God is asking His people, "Why would I give you favor or accept your offerings when you are only doing so halfheartedly?" They were sacrificing defective animals to God, animals that the governor of the land wouldn't even accept. They were expecting God to not only accept the sacrifices but to honor it and give the people favor. Now, here is a big question for you; what are you offering to God that is defective? Is it your halfhearted praise? What about your leftover money? Or even your leftover time? People of God,

I implore you to ask your Wonderful Mighty Savior to search the deep recesses of your heart and show you what is defective! Trust me; I am doing that very thing for myself. Why? Because the One who loved me first deserves no less!

Chapter 2

The Next Generation?

Judges 2:7-10 talks about the people following the Lord all the days of Joshua and all the days of the elders who outlived Joshua. After they died, another generation rose up that did not follow the Lord . . . How did this happen!? It happened in the same way it does in any generation, **they did not hear of God's Goodness and Righteousness!** They did not see the older people following God with their whole heart. They did not see the older people pray to the One that could save them. How sad is this!?

Now we have to ask ourselves some very hard questions; "How are we teaching the next generation?" "Are we showing them pride and selfishness, or, are we showing them how to love, to love even the unlovable?" "Are we showing them just how much grace and mercy our Father shows us, or, are we showing them how to have a bad attitude and how to be judgmental?" "Are we leaving it only up to our pastors and Sunday school teachers to teach these beautiful ones the Right Way, or, do we love every child of the future generation the way our God loves us?"

My fellow warriors, do not be deceived; we are called to love, to be servants, to be mothers, to be any and everything our Beautiful Savior needs us to be with every child, (young and old), not just your own. If we make the mistake of leaving it up to the pastors and Sunday school teachers to do all the work, please know this, a generation will rise up that does not know the Lord.

Don't ever let it be said of you, my wonderful friends, that the words, "It's not my job!" ever came out of your mouth.

Chapter 3

Are You Free, Free Indeed?

In Galatians four it says we are free! Free from what? We are free from sin! We are the children of the Most High, how awesome is that? My fellow warriors, why, oh why, do we act like we are the sons and daughters of peasants? Why, oh why, when we are free, free to not "have" to sin, why do we willingly go back into bondage? Imagine you are a child on the streets, stealing food just to eat, and committing crimes just to survive until you are arrested and sentenced to die. Then the King of that country came in and told you He loved you, He would die in your place and would you like to come live in His kingdom. What would you say? I would say "yes", it couldn't come out of my mouth quick enough. While you were living in His kingdom, why in the world would you ever go back on the streets and steal food, when you had all you could eat at home? Why would you commit crimes to survive, when you had the Kings army protecting you? Why do we willingly do that? Would you ever say, "I love it here, but put me back in jail. I like the feeling of being in a cage and the feeling of being in stocks?" Yet, it is done every day.

You might say to yourself, or to me, "That's crazy; who would willing put themselves back under bondage?" Let me ask you this, if God asks you to quit watching your favorite TV show, would you do it? What about wholeheartedly? Would you do it, yet grumble about it or have a bad attitude about it? What about if a friend or family member has really hurt you, and while you are praying about it, your Savior shows you a small point where you are wrong in the situation; and He wants you to go apologize to the person that hurt you so badly? Do you do it, or do you keep the anger because it is your right? I mean, they were more wrong than you were! If you do apologize, what is your attitude when you do it? (Do you notice how it all keeps coming back to attitude? We will talk later about why that is important.) Now, what do you do when Jesus tells you to go up to complete strangers and tell them, "Your Redeemer lives!"? Do you do it? I could go on and on with different situations, but I don't think that is necessary. Not only has My Beautiful Savior asked me to do those things, He has told me to do many more of them. Writing this, yeah, this is just the latest event He has told me to do, and I think I told you earlier how this is way out of my comfort zone. You know what? I do it. Why? Because I refuse to be in bondage anymore!! I am free, free indeed! If my attitude is not what it should be while doing these seemingly difficult tasks, I just bow down and ask my Wonderful, Holy, and Perfect Jesus to help me with it. Yes, friends, it's as simple as telling our Lord, "You are always right, I am always wrong. Please change my heart, better yet, Lord, put in me a New Heart to be like Yours!"

Friends, something as simple as a bad attitude, any pride in our hearts, not doing, not obeying, and not listening to the One Who Loved you first, can put you back into bondage quicker than the blink of an eye. If you have not yet fallen victim to the lies (bad attitude and pride) of the enemy, consistently ask God to guard your heart and mind from these attacks so you can recognize them when it first happens and end it before it even starts. If you *have* fallen into these traps, tell God, "Your right, I'm wrong, please fix me!" You may even fall into the category of many that I've known, including me; you believe, yet there is something, you just don't know what, that is holding you back. That's when you cry out to the One who hears, "Lord, I believe, help my unbelief!" What sweet and lovely Words. When He answers, ask Him to help make you deaf and blind to the lies and fears the enemy consistently throws your way, trying to draw you back into bondage.

My fellow warriors, make no mistake, when you willingly put yourself back in bondage, you are not free to worship, (you will be sad, depressed or sick), you are not free to read the Word, you are not free to pray, you are not free to give, to love, to tithe or to do anything that is the fruit of the Spirit. Try doing any of these things while in self-inflicted bondage. It just doesn't work.

Some may say, but Lisa, you just don't know what I'm going through. True, I don't, but God does. He is Omniscient, (all knowing), and one of the Hebrew Names for Him is El Roi, the God Who Sees. He does see your situation. He wants to help your situation. Can He get through your bad attitude to help you? (That is what I was talking about earlier, why getting rid of a bad attitude is so important, so you can hear.) Maybe, just maybe, if you ask God to change your attitude, you can then see and hear Him more clearly when He is fixing your issue. No matter what you are going through or how bad it gets, our Lord is still Righteous, Holy, Pure, Powerful, and yes friend, never forget, He is always Right!

We always ask God to change our environment. Why do we do that? We ask Him to change the people around us, to help us like them better, to make them holier. Yes, we do that. Think about the times you have asked your Savior to take the splinter out of your brothers' eye when you had a plank in your own. We've all done it. It's horrible seeing our thoughts in black and white, isn't it?

We ask God to change our business, our job, change our financial woes, we even ask Him to change our children, make them into what *we* want them to be, not what *God* wants them to be. The list just goes on and on my friend. Why don't we, instead of asking God to change our environment or the people around us, ask Him to change our, bet you've guessed it by now, attitude, about what is going on around us or the people around us. I bet if we see some of these wonderful people around us through God's eyes, we might see it's not so much them that needs to change, but us and how we interact with them. Could our "holier than thou attitude" be turning them away from their Savior. I had a person tell me several years ago, "If that is what being a Christian is all about, then I want no part of it!" Hmmm, after that, I quit asking God to change them, but change me and my horrid, mouthy attitude. In my mind this person was lazy, God just needed to change that and then the person could see just how wonderful me and God were! Well, we see how well that worked out. If you've never had a person say those words to you, you need to bow down and thank the Lord. It rips my heart today the same way it did the day it was said. At least now, though, I ask God to change me, not so much the people around me.

My fellow warriors, imagine what the world around us would be like if we were joyful, (not happy, there is a difference) while going through our tests and trials that is making us grow as Christians! Oh my, we could be a spiritual powerhouse! Isn't it worth a try?

Remember this, the Israelites wanted their circumstances changed all the time on the way to the Promised Land, go read the Word, see how they fared. Numbers chapter fourteen is where they got their death sentence.

Chapter 4

Is the World More Righteous than You?

When Israel was divided after Solomon, there was the Northern Kingdom (Israel or Ephraim) and the Southern Kingdom (Judah). Israel didn't have even one righteous (right with God) king over them. They still had prophets pleading with them to get in line with God's will, but they never had a leader that would. Now Judah did have *some* righteous kings, some more righteous than others, and some that seemed to try to provoke God to anger. Don't we act like Judah sometimes, right with God *sometimes* and provoking Him to anger other times? Provoking God, and what others see in us when we do, is what I'm going to talk about in this next paragraph or so.

In Jeremiah 3:11-13 it says unfaithful Israel is more righteous than Judah. How sad would it be Saints of God, for it to be said of you that the world is more righteous than you? Now, God is using Jeremiah to call Israel to repentance at this time, so I am mostly talking about Israel this chapter. I just had to point out that even though God is calling Israel, the one that never had a righteous king, to repentance; He felt it important to let us know that Judah had not repented wholeheartedly and was worse than Israel. Now, search your heart, have you repented wholeheartedly, turned and ran from your sin, and said, "God, You're right, I'm wrong."?

The God of this universe is pleading with Israel, saying, "Return to Me, I won't look on you with anger, My Love for you is unfailing! I won't be angry forever, *only acknowledge your guilt . . .*" Then God lists their sin. Beloved, God has already seen and made a list of your sin, He already knows. Agree with Him, turn from your ways of doing things and then . . . watch God's blessings fall on you!!! My friends, when the blessings fall, don't make the mistake of sinning again, as Israel did in the desert, by complaining that the blessing was not what you wanted nor expected. I guarantee it is definitely what you need.

Your Savior loves you so much, He will only give you what you need, and amazingly enough, sometimes that coincides with your wants. Psalms 37:4 says, "Delight yourself also in the Lord, and He shall give you the desires of your heart." My challenge to you is this, try Your Savior and see if He comes through on His promise. I know He will. Delight yourself in the Lord, and then watch the desires of your heart change. That is exactly what I did, and, praises to His Name, I got a brand new thought pattern!!

In Jeremiah 6:16-20 it says that God was again pleading with Israel to find the Good Way to walk. They said, "No, we will not walk in that way". So He sent watchmen to tell them to listen. They said, "We will not listen." Okay people of God, is your Lord telling you to do something? Is He sending people to you to try to get you to listen to Him, and if so, are you telling Him "no"? If you are saying "no", then don't be surprised when the same thing happens to you as it did Israel. Also, the offerings and sacrifices you give Him, He does not accept them until you are obedient. (1 Samuel 15:22)

Let's take a closer look at disobedience and what it actually is. When you tell the Lord "no", you are rebelling against His Word. To God, rebellion is the same thing as witchcraft. If you are being a "stiff-necked people" (or stubborn) that is equal to iniquity and idolatry. (1 Samuel 15:23)

My fellow warriors, the Holy God of this universe is talking to you! Pleading with you, "Please, do it My way! It is the best way!" Please know this; God will only plead with you for so long. Listen. Do you hear it? You know what I am talking about. That Still Small Voice you are hearing in your heart. Listen to it, because He loves you so very much. How much? So much so that He gladly took pain, punishment, humiliation and even death, so you wouldn't have to.

In Jeremiah twenty six, the Lord was telling Jeremiah to go stand in the court of the Lord's House and say to the people; if you will not listen to the Lord, walk in His Laws or listen to His prophets, then He will make your city a curse to all the nations and the House like Shi'loh. This place, Shi'loh, was a place where God's Ark of the Covenant was, but no longer is. A place where they used to worship, but no longer did. Where the Temple was, but no longer is. Are you getting the idea?

As I was reading this in Jeremiah, I couldn't help but wonder; if God got that angry over them not following Him, how much more angry must He get at us when we have seen one of the greatest Miracles of all, the God of this universe wanting to live inside of our sin filled hearts! Oh my! How much more angry must He get when His Holy Spirit is guiding us and we still say no? The Old Testament people didn't have these things. Just something to think about the next time you are seriously considering telling your Savior "no".

In Ezekiel 18:32 it says, *"For I have no pleasure in the death of one who dies," says the Lord God. "Therefore turn and live!"* Friends, God is just, righteous and Holy, He will give out deserved punishment. How many times have we seen God pleading for people to turn from their wicked ways? Why does He do this? He is Self-sufficient. As we can see, it hurts this Holy God to see a person die when they didn't need to. A thought like this, thoughts of just how much God loves me, how gracious He is, humbles me right down to my knees. I don't deserve that kind of love, and He knows I don't, yet He gladly gives it to me anyway. That pierces my heart and helps me to tell Him "yes" even when it hurts.

Chapter 5

Does Your Spirit Get the Workout It Needs?

Let me start by giving you a little history about myself. I hate talking about myself because my life seems somewhat boring, but to God, it is a masterpiece in the making. I have to be willing to endure the pain of having all that old paint, (old life), scraped away. It's thicker in some places than others; therefore, I'm more willing in some areas than others. Doesn't God want us willing *all the time?* Yes, He does. So what do I do during those times when I feel like I'm going to buckle under the pressure of the loving Hand of my Savior scraping away all the old caked on "paint"? If you expect me to say that I just tighten my halo, put on all the armor I can find and smile, (God likes cheerfulness, doesn't He?) you would be oh, so sadly mistaken.

First, I lost my halo somewhere in between a non-believer telling me they didn't want any part of Christianity because of me, and a friend at church looking at me like I had lost my mind because I was giving them this "wonderful" advice about something I knew nothing about. By the way, I hurt this person with that "wonderful" advice. Second, why would I want armor against my loving God? Third, if you can smile while being molded by God, well, He hasn't gotten to the caked on stuff yet. It's painful, yet necessary.

So what do I do? Well, sometimes, not often, I can stand and continue with some semblance of a normal life, praying for mercy all the time. Most of the time though, I just fall down and use my imagination, (God gave us that for a reason, we just misuse it most of the time.) I see myself falling into my Savior's arms and just crying. I tell Him how much it hurts, and all He says is, "I know" and I swear, I think I see a tear come to His eye too. When you are hurting, you don't have to blubber out these long prayers, just go have some quiet time with your Savior, cry in His arms and let Him soothe your hurts. Have you ever thought that maybe you don't hear from Him because you are too busy talking to hear?

Now, back to the history, (my husband, who is reading this as I write it, thinks it's hilarious when I start out with one thing and go clear around the world on a scenic journey just to get next door!). I have had one back surgery, it helped, but then the other side of my back started hurting. When I tell you that I hurt all the time, I mean, there is barely a minute in the day that I am not in some type of pain. Have you had something that you hated yet loved so dearly at the same time? While I would love to be rid of this pain, I have loved the lessons God has shown me through it. He has sent me many pearls in this ocean of pain. Would I give away this pain knowing I would give away these pearls at the same time? No. I am still in my flesh though, therefore, I do hope I can hurry these lessons up so I can be healed!

All of this started when I was in a wreck at the age of fourteen. I was driving, (don't ask, we were country people and that's just what we did), needless to say, I was inexperienced and didn't know how to drive in the rain. Anyway, I cracked my skull in two places, had a major concussion, (no light, not even dim, could touch my eyes, my mom lived in total darkness at the hospital) broke my front teeth and shattered my collar bone. The doctors didn't know if I would make it, but my Savior did. I wasn't a Christian at this time; my parents were, but not me. I was only in the hospital for a week. Now, the point of me telling you this story is God started using this horrific accident immediately, and He still is. My sister's best friend gave her life to Christ while I was in the hospital; she realized we aren't guaranteed tomorrow. Even as a non-Christian, I knew I would go through it all again for that one event. I guess that was a seed waiting to be watered and for my Savior to give the increase.

I hurt my back during that wreck, even though we didn't know that until twenty or twenty five years later. It progressively got worse. I tried walking, stretching and physical therapy to try to help my back, nothing worked. Eventually I had surgery, it helped one side, and then the other side started hurting. Tim, my husband, started doing P90X. I really like to exercise, I don't love it, but I really like it and it makes me feel better. I was jealous and would even get a bit angry because he could do this, but I couldn't. One day, about 40 lbs. later, I said enough feeling sorry for myself, I started P90X also, a much modified version. Guess what? My back felt better than it had in years and the inches started coming off. If my back was not perfect, it was, oh, so tolerable. I guess that was my first lesson in this. Instead of feeling sorry for ourselves that we can't do what others do, pick your chin up and try it, but in God's way. How many times have you ever looked at another Christian that was in God's will, saw them working for God, writing, singing, teaching and always ready to praise Him, and felt a twinge of jealousy? "Why can't I do that?" you sullenly think, "I'm a Christian too." Come on, we're family; you can admit that you have had these thoughts. I know I have. Instead of being envious, get in God's will and see what masterpiece He is going to make out of your life, I bet it will be beautiful. You may say, "Lisa, this is easy for you, you know what God's will is in your life." Yes, for now I do, but, my friend, I didn't always. When I quit telling God "no", lost my bad attitude, and shut up long enough to hear His Voice, then I knew. Until I became, "free", I didn't have a clue.

Don't forget my friends, I'm just an average person with no great talent except saying, "Here I am, Lord, pick me!"

I always wanted to sing, never could carry a note, but boy how I've always wanted to. I'm so bad, when I first started going to our church, some people wanted me to go up front to sing with them, and I declined. When they were persistent, my husband readily jumped in and said, nah, you don't want her to. And he LOVES me, he really does, bad singing voice and all. I wanted to play drums too, but I never learned how. What do you know; I get to watch my daughter be the drummer for our church. I'm so very proud of her. Now, I did have to go ahead and tell her, when she first started, that I've already asked God to reserve me a spot in the Heavenly choir as drummer. That would be awesome, if I can tear myself away from Jesus, after a few thousand years or so. My fellow warriors, you really don't have to have a great talent, just a willing heart. That's all our Holy Savior needs, or wants, to use you.

As I was working out one day, the Lord stopped me in my tracks with a second, or was it third, lesson.

In this crazy, high octane world we live in, we work so hard to get our bodies in shape, our finances in shape, our houses in shape (cause we have to keep up with the Joneses), and even our children in shape. What about our hearts and our spirits? If we worked as hard on those two things as we did these things that will one day be destroyed, think how awesome our lives would be, not to mention our relationship with our Father. Think about it, He has shown us a Love like none other, shouldn't we show Him the love and respect He deserves, not just one or two days a week, but *every* single day these frail bodies draw breath?

One day in Sunday School, before the Lord called me to be a Sunday School teacher, I was in the adult class and told them that I *wanted* to have a closer walk with God, but didn't know how nor did I have the will. I don't mind admitting my shortcomings to other Christians; it will hopefully get more people to pray for this horrible sinner. God already knows my faults, if I could hide them from anyone, it would be Him. That just doesn't work out too well, so, since I can't hide from the One who matters, I need all the prayers I can get. Anyway, back to wanting to have a closer walk with God. When I told them this, a friend of Tim's told me, well, here's what you do; every morning, when you wake up, just ask God "What can I do to glorify You today, Lord?" That sounds easy, right? Well, that *was* easy, it's the doing it that isn't. That's when you have to be willing to get out of your comfort zone.

Right after this, I was jogging, (before I realized I shouldn't) around the community track while listening to my iPod and praising my Savior. God told me to go up to some strangers that I would see every now and again walking, and tell them, "Your Redeemer lives!" I said, "But God, I don't know them." God replied, "I don't care, **go** tell them that their Redeemer lives." I pleaded with God, "But God, I don't know them!" He didn't say another word. Complete silence. If you think God gave up at this time, you would be so very wrong! All of a sudden I couldn't breathe, I couldn't run, could barely walk. Hmmm, who do you think walked by at that very moment? Yep, the people I didn't know; complete strangers to me. I heard God loud and clear. I squeaked out, "Your Redeemer lives . . ." They smiled politely and said, "Yes, He does." I never saw them at the track again. I got the point, God did that for me, not just them. He loved me so much; He wouldn't let me stay where I was comfortable. He wanted to see me grow, stretch my wings and show me all the things He could accomplish through me if I would only have an obedient heart.

Another lesson I've learned, is that sometimes, we are in so much pain, physically and/or spiritually that no amount of "working out" is going to help. What do you do then? Well, my friend, I've been there numerous times with my back issues. Most of the time I praise God for loving me so much and trusting me to follow Him no matter what the evil one throws my way. Sometimes, sometimes, I just crawl in bed and cry. I cry out to Jehovah Rapha, (the Lord our Healer). You know what, every once in a while, we need to be like children, crawl into our Saviors arms, cry and let Him soothe our hurts. It's okay, He loves when we are that dependent on Him, He loves when we trust Him that much. Go ahead, child of God, crawl into His lap, and cry out your hurts. Let Him hug you, kiss your forehead and tell you He will take care of it. He will, in His time. His time is not like our time . . . it may be faster, it may be slower. Know this, it will be perfect timing.

I was in church a couple of Sundays ago and was talking with my Lord. I wasn't whining, I wasn't angry; maybe I was looking for assurance. I asked God, "Lord, You have healed so many people, I've watched my dad come through numerous heart surgeries, pneumonia and mushroom poisoning (look that one up, very, very few survive). So many people in our church have been healed, why not me, Lord? I know You love me and You would just tell me if I was preventing it from happening, so why not me?" The answer I got pierced my heart to the core. A joy came to me like none other and I couldn't stem the flow of tears. He answered me and said, "I have healed you, from the worst disease known to mankind, your sinful heart." My friends, that shook me to the core, He was right. What does it matter if I have to go through a few aches and pains? **I am healed,** and hopefully, I can glorify my Father's Name while going through these aches and pains.

Chapter 6

How Well do You Know Your Enemy?

Why is it important to know your enemy? If you don't know what tactics he uses, you won't know how to prepare for them, and you won't see him coming. I know, without a doubt, that when I do something that the Lord has asked me to do, or when I have done something to glorify God, I *know* that I am going to get attacked. Do you think I am just going to sit there and allow myself to get beaten up? No, I am going to go ahead and start praying, asking my Savior to protect me.

Do you know how many times I have heard someone say "Satan can't get me, I will do such and such, and kick him down!" Really? Well, if we can do that, why did our Lord tell his disciples, "Watch and pray, lest you enter into temptation. The spirit is willing, but the flesh is weak." (Matt. 26:41) Why would the Lord tell us, "Be sober, be vigilant; because your adversary the devil walks about like a roaring lion, seeking whom he may devour?" (1 Pet. 5:8) I know this, I am not stronger than satan, I am not smarter than him, nor am I more powerful, but, my Father is. Praise His Name, my Father can do *any and everything!* So why do we try to still battle satan in our own power? My friend, quit trying to battle satan on your own or in the flesh, you will lose every time. When you let God go before you in battle, you will always win. It may not be the victory you want, or the victory you thought it would be, but it is still a win, a victory. The Israelites didn't think Jesus was their Messiah either, and they were not expecting that type of victory. They wanted a victorious Messiah to come riding in on a horse with a sword. The disciples didn't think the Cross was their victory, they thought it was their end. When they had their spiritual eyes opened by their Savior in a tightly closed up room where they were hiding, then they knew just what a victory the Cross was.

I was driving down the road one day, coming home from grocery shopping, I think, and an eighteen wheeler was passing me. At that moment the thought hit me, satan would love to throw my car in front of that truck. He hates me, and all he wants to do is destroy me, because I belong to his archenemy, God. I have read the Word, (Job, to be precise) so I know satan has to go before God to get permission to do anything to me. Guess what? My car didn't get thrown before that truck. If he actually asked my Father for that, well, He must have said "No". I wonder how many times satan has went before God concerning us and been told "No?" Hmmm, maybe, just maybe, instead of whining and crying over the few tests, trials, or tribulations we go through, why don't we thank our Lord and praise His Name for the ones He saves us from.

Friends, I have heard of, seen, and listened to people with debilitating diseases or has cancer that is going through chemo, praising God the whole time. They know that even though they are sick, sicker than most of us could only imagine, God and God alone is still worthy to be praised! Yet, if we don't get the car we want, do not have money to buy a bigger house or can't even scrape together change to go out to dinner and a movie, we whine and cry instead of praising His name for all the blessings He does give us. Now, I won't get into the reasons why it's possible you can't afford those things or even things you need, I will have to leave that up to my husband. He is the financial guru of our church and has looked up scripture after scripture on tithing and the blessings from it. We may have to get him to write a book or teach some classes on God and money, he would be wonderful at it.

It is human nature to pity ourselves when we hurt. Whew! Praise God! He gave us a new nature! Ask God to gently remind you to quit grumbling over the few trials you have been chosen to go through, trials picked just for you to, to make you stronger. He will, but only if you are going to listen. He won't waste His time telling you to do something that He already knows you aren't going to do. I am talking to myself, also, when I am writing this stuff. The harsher I sound, most likely means it is probably something I know I need to overcome also.

Yesterday morning, I got up, giving myself the grandest pity party of them all. I whined to God,

"I'm hurting God, can't I just get out of reading the Bible today, I'll read it tomorrow." Oh, how my back was hurting. I had my phone right there beside me, with the Bible downloaded on it. God reminded me of that. So I whined a little louder, "But God, I don't remember what chapters I'm reading." (I read five chapters a morning, unless God tells me different, two History, one Poetry, one Prophet and one New Testament.) So God reminds me, all five chapters where I stopped at were brought to mind. Hmm, here was my choice, 1) continue with the pity party or option 2) take the gift my Father gave me and rejoice that He loves me so much. I chose option two, not in my own power, but in the power He so lovingly gives us all, if we will just use it.

I have heard many, many people say, "I don't know if God is talking to me or not" or "I can't tell who is talking to me, God or satan." Well, I think all Christians have been there at one point or another, myself included. I know how frustrating that can be; you just want God to tell you which way to go, what to do or what to say. The first thing I would say is, get to know your Savior.

If you want to know about someone famous, what do you do? You do like all other Americans, Google it or go to the library and see if they have a biography written about them, and then you read it. Read God's Word, He didn't give it to us to see how holy we can look with it on our coffee table, or carrying it to church. He gave it to us because He wants us to be holy. 1 Peter 1:16 says; *because it is written, "Be holy, for I am holy."* My friends, read the Word, pray to a holy Savior. Imagine, the God of this universe is sitting on His throne, anxiously waiting to hear from His beloved, you. If you don't talk to Him or read about Him, how are you going to know His voice? John 10:3-5 *"To him the doorkeeper opens, and the sheep hear his voice; and he calls his own sheep by name and leads them out. (4)And when he brings out his own sheep, he goes before them; and the sheep follow him, for they know his voice. (5) Yet they will by no means follow a stranger, but will flee from him, for they do not know the voice of strangers."* My friends, the more you fellowship with the Father, the more you know Him, and, the more you know Him, the more you will recognize a voice that is not His.

Holy Ones, as you immerse yourself in the love of God and read His word, you will see that He tells you about the enemy. He wants you to know the enemy, and know his tactic. You have also been given a battle plan, all through the Word. Read it for yourself, you just can't go wrong. You may even do a 180 and be right, with God.

Chapter 7

Is God Really First in Your Life?

This is probably going to be the hardest chapter for me to write. This is because I am still witnessing some of the destruction I have caused. I've always said God came first, since I've been a Christian. I mean, I have fallen away, was chastised, and came back, halfheartedly. God always got me in the end, and that's the part I like. Like I said, I would always say God came first in my life. I was a liar, until now.

When I first became a Christian at the age of twenty eight, I asked God first; to be a missionary and second; to allow me to see what a Christian marriage was like here on earth, before I went home. I got both prayers answered, just not in the way I thought. It really is quite humorous. I went to my God given mission field, Louisiana National Guard

Youth Challenge Program, as a Cadre. A cadre is like a drill sergeant for at risk youths. Definitely not the mission I was expecting, but if I would have told God "no" to that first answered prayer, I wouldn't have gotten the answer to my second. Who do you think I would meet while I was training for this job? Yep, my future Christian husband. Problem, he wasn't a Christian at the time and I hated him. God really does have a sense of humor; I live it all the time. I also love it all the time.

This man that God would ensure I marry, through many humorous events had a beautiful daughter. I was scared of that; I didn't have children of my own. How was I going to help raise a child that was sure to hate the evil stepmother? So, I do what I always do when I get scared, I pray to the One who isn't afraid. I asked Him to put a love in my heart for this child that I didn't know, like no other love I had known before. That was the third answered prayer. Now, don't get me wrong, it was a nightmare at first, but I still had a love that couldn't go away. My Father had put it in my heart, how could it. I know she is my step-daughter legally, but try to tell my heart that, it would reject that statement as a lie out of the pits of hades. My heart says she is the child God gave me that my "Mom's" heart has longed for. Tim and I have tried so hard to bring her up the way we think God would want us to, not how we think it should be done, or so I thought.

This is where my heart is still a bit fragile. My husband is a penny pincher and very frugal. He is also very practical. Madison wanted a Facebook account but Tim said she was too young. I bugged him, for her, until he gave in. He didn't think we should pay so much money on school clothes. I wanted her to have popular ones so she would fit in. I bugged him until he gave in. He said she didn't need a cell phone; I came up with every excuse in the book of why she did and kept on until he gave in. Madison knew she could always come to me to talk her dad into anything. I thought I was doing a good job, I mean, Madison had given her heart to the Lord, she was a great kid, and we got along great, we loved each other, and I thought she would *never* come to love me.

I won't tell Madison's story, it's not mine to tell, but I will tell mine. Some events happened that devastated us, and scared us, through Madison. The main thing that scared us was she was talking to people online that she didn't know, on a smart phone, which had GPS. We still have no clue who she was talking to, but we do know who is going to protect her, better than we ever could. She had fallen far away from God; she even admitted that she had been pretending, for our sakes and the churches, to want to follow God. It all started shortly after the clothes and cell phone thing.

I was praying for Madison shortly after this, a prayer I'm sure many mother's has and will pray. My Lord, ever so gently, told me that the mess Madison had gotten herself into was partly my fault. I was devastated. I asked Him how. He brought back to mind all the passages in His Word that told me how He said I should treat my husband, a husband that He blessed me with, not one that I deserved. Let's look at a few; Ephesians 5:22-24 *Wives, submit to your own husbands, as to the Lord. (23) For the husband is head of the wife, as also Christ is head of the church; and He is the Savior of the body. (24) Therefore, just as the church is subject to Christ, so let the wives be to their own husbands in everything.* Colossians 3:18 *Wives, submit to your own husbands, as is fitting in the Lord.* 1 Peter 3:1-4 *Wives, likewise, be submissive to your own husbands, that even if some do not obey the word, they, without a word, may be won by the conduct of their wives, (2) when they observe your chaste conduct accompanied by fear. (3) Do not let your adornment be merely outward—arranging the hair, wearing gold, or putting on fine apparel—(4) rather let it be the hidden person of the heart, with the incorruptible beauty of a gentle and quiet spirit, which is very precious in the sight of God.*

I don't know about you, ladies, but as for me, I *truly*, with every fiber of my being, want to be precious in the sight of God. As I was typing out these verses, my heart was again broken, seeing all the ways that I fail to obey His Word. I will continue to try to remedy that, with my Savior's help. I know I can't do it in my own power.

Back to God telling me how I was partly to blame. I'm sure you can see it by now, but I feel I have to confess my sins before you, hoping you don't commit the same ones and have to live with the guilt I live with today. If God has told me to be submissive to my husband in *everything*, yet, if I continued to bug Tim, when he truly felt in his heart that all those things were wrong for Madison, wasn't I, in essence, disobeying God? And if I was doing all of this for Madison, disobeying God, then ultimately I was putting Madison before God. How could I do that? I love God, with my whole heart, I love Tim, as God wants me to, and I love and adore this beautiful child God blessed me with. How could I damage all three of these relationships this way? Easy, I was ever so subtlety deceived by satan, just as he deceived Eve. Why should he change tactics, when it still works so well today? (This is just another reason why you need to know your enemy and his tactics).

The main thing I want you to take away from this is; if you love someone, love them soooo much, that you would never put them before God. They don't deserve to have that position, and if they love God, I guarantee, they don't *want* that position in your life.

Now ladies, I have to add this, because if any of you are like I was, you are bristling somewhat from the verses I put in here. When I first married Tim, I really wanted to be a Godly wife, so I looked up all the verses I could find. I had been praying before we got married for help in this, I had a whole year to get myself ready to be the wife God wanted me to be. I got to Ephesians 5:33. The second part . . . *"let the wife see that she respects her husband."* I wanted to really know about this, so I looked in different versions of the Bible. The King James Version used "reverence" instead of "respect". I knew what those words meant, but I wanted to be sure on reverence, so I looked at the Greek definition. When I read, "to be in awe of", ladies, I almost threw the book across the room. Everything in me said, "**noooo, I will not be like that**, God, you are wrong on this one, you can't possibly want me to think like that!" Then I got the two-by-four in the head. God ever so gently asked me, "Do you really think I'm wrong?" I started crying, sobbing really, and said, "God, I know you're right, but I can't help how I feel." Like lightning, the answer came, "ask God to change my way of thinking into His way of thinking and my feelings would change along with it". It's true, when I prayed that prayer, my feeling changed immediately! Feelings are fickle; they just go along with what the brain tells them. My dad gave me some of the most wonderful advice when I was younger, still a non-Christian, but it stuck with me anyway. "If you don't love someone, act like you do, and eventually, you will." Some of the best advice

I've ever gotten. If you don't "feel like" you love God, obey Him, and the feelings will follow. James 1:22 *But be doers of the word, and not hearers only, deceiving yourselves.*

Chapter 8

Are You Trying to be God's Puppet?

When I was just a babe in Christ I went through a phase that I have heard called the "honeymoon" stage. I wanted to please God in everything I did, not that I don't now, but it was different then.

You know how you are when you first get married, don't you? We do things way out of our ordinary ways to try to please our new spouse. Me, I took the saying "the way to a man's heart is through his stomach" to a whole new level. I think we gained twenty pounds each in the first year. We shop, cook, clean, do everything, to try to please our new spouse. We know the real us, and we are scared for them to know that we, too, have bad breath in the morning, and that it takes tons of work to look like the woman they dated, then married. We are scared for them to know that we, dare I say it, have smelly bodily functions just like the rest of every other human alive. We are scared that they won't love us as much as they used to. So, we try to cover it all up, for a minute. Then, we get tired of all the work it takes to not be us. The gigs up, it's do or die, will they still love us? The honeymoon is over. The stars we once had in our eyes for our beloved, is down to the last one and the fuel is running pretty low on it. We still love them, but we have found out, oh my, we married a human and *they are not perfect!* We even want to punch them every now and again for just how human they are. That love is still there. Not an emotion, remember, love is not an emotion, it's an act. Goodness, no, we are not feeling an emotion, but a deep desire to continue on this path with this other non-perfect specimen.

Well, we get that way with God too. The stars are gone out of our eyes; the newness of the relationship is gone. Now what? It is sooo very sad to say, this is where a lot of people jump ship. If they only knew what they were going to miss out on later, the golden years, because we are on the verge of going to the next stage, the most difficult one, teen years. The teen years I believe are the most painful, in the physical world and the spiritual world. I think this stage is the most essential. This is where we do most of our growing, but is also when we go through tremendous amounts of pain. God told us what to expect. Read 1 John: 2.

It is at this time, (the honeymoon is over, teen years, whatever you prefer to call it), that I found it so very easy to give in to my inner man. It was so easy to just fall back into some of my old ways. I didn't know it at the time, (I do now, because I got to know my enemy), but satan was standing by just waiting to pounce. What happened, did God leave me, I was so protected before? No, my friend, He never left, in fact He never moved a muscle. He was doing what He had to do, I had reached preteen, I had to stretch my wings. How could I grow otherwise?

You have seen the parents that do every single little thing for their children, protect them from every bump and bruise that comes their way, physically and emotionally and therefore never allow them to grow into self-sufficient adults. What happens to them when they face the world without their parents there to take care of everything? Well, they don't make it very well; they are devastated at the least little bump. God loves us; He wants to toughen us up a bit. If He doesn't allow that to happen, what are we going to do when we get into a disagreement with someone at church? Leave? Ok, that's an option, until the next church you go to has a person that you disagree with. Then what? Guys, we have to be tough, have thick skin, because we are going to have disagreements in church, we have a very powerful enemy that is going to ensure that! So, instead of shielding us, our loving Father teaches how to deal with it. He teaches us how to deal with all the situations that come our way, not shield us from all of them, otherwise, where would freewill come into play and how would we grow into the mature Christian that our loving Father wants us to be? Sure, who wouldn't choose the option of no trials, tribulations or attacks from the enemy? The churches would be packed every Sunday if following God ensured that. Dear ones, God wants us to love Him no matter what! Why shouldn't we? He loved us "no matter what." Oh, how He loved us, when He should have just destroyed us because of our wicked ways.

Anyway, it was during this time, when I found myself having choices, I would always make the wrong one. Oh, how I **wanted** to do good, but I never seemed to.

The words of Paul never felt more real to me than at this time. (Romans 7:14-15; 7:21-25) *For we know that the law is spiritual, but I am carnal, sold under sin. (15) For what I am doing I do not understand. For what I will to do, that I do not practice; but what I hate, that I do.—(21) I then find a law, that evil is present with me, the one who wills to do good. (22) For I delight in the law of God according to the inward man. (23) But I see another law in my members, warring against the law of my mind, and bringing me into captivity to the law of sin which is in my members. (24) O wretched man that I am! Who will deliver me from this body of death? (25) I thank God—through Jesus Christ our Lord!* My friends, I hated living in this sinful body and I didn't realize it at the time, but, God wasn't done with me yet, praise to His Holy Name!!

While I was trying to find my way, I remember crying out to God, "My Lord, why won't You just make me do the right thing! I am using my freewill; I want You to take over, completely, just for Your purposes." Oh, how easy that would have been, just to be puppet-like and always doing the right thing, never disappointing the One that I loved so much, yet it would have been a very shallow relationship, it wouldn't have substance. God loved me so much; He wanted a deep rooted relationship that couldn't be shaken. I am so thankful for His tough love now. Now that I am in this deep rooted relationship, I can see why God longed for this, and beloved, He longs for that relationship with you too. I have to say this, I am still amazed and in total awe that the God of this universe, the Creator of all things longed for any type of relationship with me. I know what I was like before, *I* didn't want a relationship with me, why would He? My friend, He could see Himself in me when I couldn't.

In Hebrews chapters five and six the author is writing a letter to the Hebrews because when some of them should be teaching younger Christians, they had to be fed "milk" themselves because they had not grown any and were unskilled in the word of righteousness. He goes on to write that "solid food" belongs to those of full age, those who have worked out their spiritual muscles, read the Word, stayed in prayer and had their senses exercised and could discern both good and evil. He also says to leave the elementary principle of Christ, and let's go on to perfection. Is he saying we are going to reach the level of being perfect while on this earth? No. But that does not mean we should stop striving for it, don't you want to look (I'm not talking physically) and act as much like your Savior as possible?

Have you read 1 John:2 yet? (I cannot stress enough, *do not take my word for it, read it for yourself.*) I believe there are a few reasons why God wanted us to know about the different states of maturity. First, so you know what He expects of you. Second, God doesn't' want you to try and skip levels. Have you ever heard of a two year old, that had just been potty trained, run and jump into the car and tell his parents, "Ok, mom, dad, I'm ready to drive, need to go get my girl for our date"? Well, that's just absurd! Then why do we have babes in Christ trying to skip the growing and maturing years and trying to be mature Christians that they are neither capable nor equipped to be? Again, I know, and so does your Savior, that these are the most difficult years to get through and it feels like they will never end, but they will, and I promise, your Savior has not left nor will He. He has too much love for you, a love that wants a deep rooted relationship.

The third reason is so you can see that there is great hope of what the future holds for the Christian that stays on the path Christ intended. We are going to look a little more into this hope in a minute. Let's go over what John says about this in 1 John 2:12-14.

12) I write to you little children,
>> Because your sins are forgiven you for His name's sake.

13) I write to you, fathers,
>> Because you have known Him who is from the beginning.
> I write to you, young men,
>> Because you have overcome the wicked one.
> I write to you, little children,
>> Because you have known the Father.

14) I have written to you, fathers,
>   Because you have known Him who is
>   from the beginning.
> I have written to you, young men.
>   Because you are strong and the word of
>   God abides in you,
>   And you have overcome the wicked one.

Can you see it, the hope? The little children are promised their sins are forgiven, and they know the Father. The fathers, the mature Christians, **know** the One who is from the beginning. They are settled, they have their unshakable roots, and they have a love for their Savior that no trial or tribulation can uproot. Isn't that what everybody looks forward to, the golden years? Now, let's look at the growing years. What have the young men been promised? They have learned to overcome the wicked one, they are strong and the word of God is in them. Oh, my friends, how can you get to the golden years if you haven't learned any self-control, or how to read the Word daily or even how to stay in contact, pray, with the Father daily? This is where the bulk of Christian living is taught. Now, don't get me wrong, we will never stop learning and growing, but we be less shaken, a bit calmer, if you will, when things come our way that are out of our control.

I can hear some of you saying right now, "well, Lisa, you don't have to go through what I'm going through and it's easy for you to say this, you have gotten through it." Yes I have, and you know what, when I was going through the "teen" years, I said the exact same thing. You are going to make it, you will learn to overcome the wicked one and he is already trembling in his boots thinking about it. Just remember, it is more about attitude toward sin and not as much about our failures. ". . . *The effective, fervent prayer of a righteous man avails much."* James 5:16b

A little more on this hope, if you are wanting God to just take over and completely control your life, puppet-like, guess what? It is possible. The more you obey God, the more of your life that you give over to Him, the more He controls you. An example would be, when I first became a Christian, I was put to a test on tithing. Praise to God, I passed, I was a first time go! I was so excited, I honestly didn't have too many temptations where money was concerned, still don't. I gave that part of me over to God from the beginning. I had a long way to go, though, on controlling the tongue. I've just learned that one in the past couple of years. Now God has control of that part of my life. I had issues with selfishness with my time, ummm, I'm still working on that area, but God is gently and slowing taking over that area. That is just a few, very few, examples of what I mean.

Let's look at it this way, if another country, say, Canada, wanted to come over and take control of the USA, how would they do it? It would be difficult to take control of all the states at one time, but, let's say they start with Maine, they get control of Maine and occupy that state. We have lost that area of our country, they control it. Then they move into New Hampshire, they take control of that area, we have lost control of another part of our country. They move onto Vermont, then Massachusetts, then Rhode Island and take control, one by one, all the states in America. That would make it more possible. Well, God can and will move in and take control of each area of our lives, if we allow Him too. He won't rush in and try to take control of all the areas in our lives at one time, just one state at a time. Any more than that, we wouldn't be able to withstand the onslaught. As simple as that, God can control your entire life. Notice that I did not say "as easy as that", though it may be simple, my friend, it will never be easy. It is human nature to want to fight back something or someone trying to invade our space. Again, I'm so very thankful God gives us a new nature. Just allow the Holy Spirit to invade; the more willing you are, the less painful it will be.

Chapter 9

Who Are You Yoked With?

We have all heard, hopefully lived, and quoted (probably more than we've lived it) the well-known verse in 2 Corinthians 6:14 *"Do not be unequally yoked together with unbelievers. For what fellowship has righteousness with lawlessness? And what communion has light with darkness?"* Yes, we have quoted that verse so much that it seems to have lost its effect on non-believers. We also equate that verse to marriage and marriage only. Oh, my fellow Christians, don't quit reading, the first part of verse 16 says, *"And what agreement has the temple of God with idols? For you are the temple of the living God . . ."* Now, my friends, if you are the temple of God, doesn't that mean that God goes with you wherever you are? Do you honestly think the Holy, Pure, and Righteous God of this universe wants to be yoked to or teamed up with an idol worshipper as a friend or as a business partner? When we decide that a non-Christian will make a good partner in marriage, business, or as a friend, what we are essentially doing is yoking ourselves to an idol worshipper. You may say, "Now, Lisa, I would never do that, they don't have idols they bow down to, I have even seen them at church on Easter and Christmas!"

Let's define idol worshipping. The encyclopedia Britannica[1] says it is "the worship of someone or something other than God as though it was God." Now, God says that if you put anything before Him, it is an idol. Do these non-Christians that you are yoked with put anything before God? I'm sure they do, they haven't been taught by the Holy Spirit how not to.

In Deut. 22:10 it tells us not to plow an ox and a donkey together. I wonder why? Well, I did a little research. What I read was, the ox is much stronger than the donkey and they couldn't plow

---

1   "idolatry." britannica.com. Britannica Online Encyclopedia, 2013 Web. 10 April 2013

at the same speed. The ox has the strength but the donkey has more speed, therefore, the oxen would suffer greatly, all the weight would be put on him. The donkey ate poisonous weeds and had horrid breath from it; therefore the ox would plow with one shoulder, so it could keep his head turned away from the donkey. My friends, you could be hurt, spiritually, mentally, and emotionally if you yoke yourself to an unbeliever. You would have to breathe in horrid poisons from the non-believer, even if it smells sweet. That is the way the enemy works. Sin can look, smell, and feel oh, so sweet, until you figure out, you smelled poisonous weeds all this time. Trust the Lord, He has your best interest at heart, and even if you can't see it at the moment, He sees the destruction at the end of the road.

The Lord has said not to mix linen and wool in Deut. 22:11. This seems irrelevant, but once you do a little research, you will find that when you mix the two it can increase the power of passing off electricity from the body. I read that it has something to do with the wool shedding electrons, and the linen pushing the electrons off and continuing on that cycle. All that being said, mixing the two in a very hot climate can exhaust your strength and cause blisters. I guess the purpose of telling you this is to say, even though something in the Bible may not make sense to you, listen to God anyway, He is so much wiser and intelligent than we could ever be. Also, how exhausting do you think it would be to try to live for Christ and have someone nagging you every single day of your life to try to get you to stop?

Please, my fellow Christians, think long and hard about the consequences of yoking yourself to a non-Christian or, in some circumstances, a Christian from a different denomination than yours. In either case, you don't think the same, and each other's words will be like poison and exhaust your strength and cause very uncomfortable situations. God told us to not be unequally yoked for a reason; He loves us and wants the best for us. Jeremiah 29:11 says, *"For I know the thoughts that I think toward you, says the Lord, thoughts of peace and not of evil, to give you a future and a hope."*

Chapter 10

Do You Try to Clean Yourself Up Before Coming to God?

I was on the way to church the other day with my husband and daughter. Madison was telling us about her lesson in Sunday school the week before. The teacher had a bucket, water, and a towel; she was going to wash their feet. She would only wash the teenager's feet that wanted her to, and she didn't force them. Madison didn't want her feet washed. I asked her why and she said because she had not cleaned her feet up, (they were clean, but she hadn't had a pedicure). I asked her why would that matter, that the Lord is pleased with us when we can humble ourselves enough to allow someone to wash our feet. She still insisted she would have allowed it had she gotten a pedicure. My question to her was, "So, do you have to clean yourself up before you go to Jesus?" Of course, like many other fifteen year olds, she got frustrated and said, "No, but it's not the same!" I pointed out to her, as gently as I could, that it was the sin of pride standing in her way by not allowing her teacher to wash her feet under any circumstances. Naturally, she told me that was not the issue. Her dad then piped in, "So, Madison, you know what the Bible says, you just don't want to follow it?" Needless to say, the frustration mounted. I just asked her to pray over the issue. Now that I have told my child's pride issue, I have to say, having someone wash my feet would be one of the hardest things for me to do.

Servitude? Not an issue for me, I could wash a hundred feet and not have a problem with it at all, could even smile the whole time I was doing it. Ahhh, here it comes, shouldn't we be able to humble ourselves enough to allow people to do something for us or ask for help? A lot of us Christians have a hard time with that. I know because I'm one of them. Yet, I will throw up at someone, "Please, allow me to help, don't take my blessings away!!!" My fellow warriors, I mean that, with all my heart. Then why am I (or we) taking other peoples blessings away?

Now, Madison said she wouldn't have an issue with having her feet washed if she could have gotten a pedicure first. Well, she is doing better than me, I would have an issue no matter what, but I would try very hard to go with it. When she said that, I started thinking, how many times has satan lied to people and told them they couldn't go to God as they were, they needed to clean their act up a little? All of us have fallen for that at some point in our life. The evil one wants you to think you are unfit, too dirty or even worse, God would not accept you unless you got a "pedicure" first. What a lie that is! If we try to clean ourselves up, it is futile. It won't last. It all goes back to two verses that I have heard my dad quote thousands of times, Ephesians 2:8-9, *"For by grace you have been saved through faith, and that not of yourselves; it is the gift of God, (9) not of works, lest anyone should boast."* You cannot do enough work to please God. Romans 8: 7-8 *"Because the carnal mind is enmity against God; for it is not subject to the law of God, nor indeed can be. (8) So then, those who are in the flesh cannot please God."* If you truly want a lasting change in your life/ lifestyle, then go to God and let Him *"wash you white as snow."* When He does this, don't fall for the lie that this change, this salvation, isn't real. I used to do that all the time, until I heard someone say one day that for me to not believe I am saved, I am calling God a liar! Romans 8:16 *"The Spirit Himself bears witness with our spirit that we are children of God,"* Let that verse comfort you when the enemy comes in to lie to you.

People, yes, we are saved by grace, but, does that mean that we have a license to sin? God forbid! No! But it does give us a license to not` live under the bondage of condemnation of our past sins. Again, it's about that attitude. What is yours toward sin? If you are heartbroken over your sin, turn to your Savior and let Him do the work in you that only He can do. If you have a flippant attitude over your sin, my friend, maybe you need to check your relationship with the Holy God of this universe. The last part of Philippians 2:12 says, *"work out your own salvation with fear and trembling;"*

Chapter 11

Are You a Mary or a Martha?

I am going to follow the Word, *"Confess your trespasses to one another, and pray for one another, that you may be healed."* James 5: 16. I will confess in a bit, but let's read the story of Mary and Martha first. Luke 10:38-42 says, *"Now it happened as they went that He entered a certain village; and a certain woman named Martha welcomed Him into her house. (39) And she had a sister called Mary, who also sat at Jesus' feet and heard His word. (40) But Martha was distracted with much serving, and she approached Him and said,* **"Lord, do You not care that my sister has left me to serve alone? Therefore tell her to help me."** *(41) And Jesus answered and said to her,* **"Martha, Martha, you are worried and troubled about many things. (42) But one thing**

is needed, and Mary has chosen that good part, which will not be taken away from her."

Back to my confession, I have found that I have not worked on this awesome project (my book) that my Father has so wondrously given me, in about one and a half to two months. It may have been longer, I don't know. That is how easily we can be deceived, time passes and we don't realize it's been a week since we have prayed or a month since we have fellowshipped, a year since we have given our whole self, (heart and soul) to the Lord. It's scary how that happens. Christmas has just passed and I am just now awakened from the deception I have been under. I tell you this so you will pray for me. Even though this is in the past, it could come up again in the future for whatever God has in store for me.

Right around Thanksgiving, I found myself busier than I have ever been in my entire life. You may say, "Really, Lisa, don't you think you are exaggerating just a bit . . ." No, my friend, I'm not. I haven't had time to take care of my family. I think I can count on one hand how many times I have cooked for my family in the last two months, and I normally cook every night! It is cost efficient; I like being a good steward of the money God has given my husband and me. It is healthier; I want to treat this body with respect, by not eating unhealthy fast food all the time, because God loves me, all of me. Finally, I want to put others, my family, before myself; take time to cook for them, because God puts me first all the time.

Yes, it was getting close to Christmas, so naturally, everybody was busier, but this was different. I was cooking for the church, helping out with other things within the church. I was taking care of my mom and dad, running to town for my daughter, my husband, and any other poor soul that needed anything. I elected myself, to help the other busy people in the church, to take charge and do all the Christmas shopping for the family we raised money for in the church. During all of this, I am working, a lot. I love my job, I love helping in the church, and I love taking care of my parents. I love all the things I was doing.

Now that you have read most of the things that was keeping my busy, doesn't sound like anything was wrong, does it? I was working for the Lord, and really, that is never wrong, is it? If it was coming between mine and His fellowship, it was. Boy was it. Satan couldn't come at me with "worldly" things to keep me busy, nah, I've been doing this too long, and he knows it, I wouldn't fall for that. Don't underestimate your enemy, remember, and get to know him!

I hadn't felt the presence of God in weeks. Now, I've told you, and I firmly stand by it, I don't go on feelings, my enemy knows this too. Therefore, that was just a little ding on the warning bell. I started putting things before my Bible reading in the morning, because it was "time and God efficient" to listen to an audio Bible while I was fixing my hair or whatever else I needed to do personal wise to leave the house. That began because on several mornings, my day got started the second I rolled out of bed, no time to sit and drink coffee and read the Word. I would wait till I was getting ready to listen to the Word. Now, I do hear a bit better, it soaks in, for me personally if I am not idle, so an audio Bible is better for me. Wasn't it wonderful of God to provide that for me for those days that started so early and I can't have a day without hearing His wonderful Word? It all seems perfectly harmless, until I started a day where I had thirty or so minutes to kill before having to start getting ready to leave the house. I started my day reading the newspaper; it was okay though, because I hear better when I am not idle, I just knew God understood that. Then, one night I was getting ready for bed, oh, my . . . a horrid reminder passed through my head. I hadn't read the Bible that day. Oh, well, God understood, I have been so horribly busy and I was so tired, I couldn't concentrate to read that late, I would pick back up in the morning. Next day, same thing, I listened to the Bible, but not until I was getting ready to leave, (satan knew to not pull the same trick too soon, I would catch on). Another day came that I forgot to listen/read the Bible, I squeezed it in that afternoon when I had about five minutes of spare time. Then another day came along where I forgot to read the Word altogether, again. Still, by this time though, my spirit had the beginnings of a callous on it, so it was again, just a ding on the warning bell, I barely heard it. Oh, how clever and deceptive our enemy is, everything I was doing was for God, what could possibly be wrong?

At this point, I have to give a shout out to my mom; I have the best mom in the whole world. I was shopping with her, we were just running around town, and I told her that I didn't feel right with God. She warned me that satan would try to make me feel that way, try to get me to worry, therefore, get me off track. I told her that I wasn't feeling guilty, but somewhat uncomfortable in my spirit. Her response was simple, "ooh, that's not good, you might want to check on that." I truly love my mom's bluntness. When it comes to her Lord, she does not mess around or try to make you feel good. So, now I knew, something wasn't right. Do I just ignore it, or ask God what was going on. I love God, so I asked Him what was wrong. That Still Small Voice spoke, again, and told me that He wasn't first in my life. If you haven't figured it out yet, I did try to put up a feeble argument. I said, "Lord, you know I love you and you are first!" It was almost like a movie projector, the past several weeks playing over and over, how I didn't give God the first part of my day, how busyness and my need for convenience took first seat. My heart broke, I repented and the next day God came first along with every day since. Guess what, God added a few more chapters to my daily Bible reading. Now, not only do I read five chapters in the morning, but also when I am doing busy work, in the kitchen, getting ready, or wherever I might be and can hear His word and absorb it. I love it! That's God for you, when you obey, He may add more work for you but it won't seem like work, He will allow you to love it. Isn't He like no other, this awesome Savior we serve.

Now if you didn't see it, let me point it out, I was being a Martha and pushing God aside. You might be asking, don't we need Martha's? I will answer you with a big fat **yes**, but, not to the point of losing the Mary inside of you. My fellow warriors, you can't just be a Mary, which leaves all the work for everybody else. Let's try to find that healthy balance. Jesus said in Mark ten that if anyone wants to become great, they will become your servant. Jesus was not contradicting Himself in the Scriptures, He was telling Martha that while her service was needful and wonderful in His eyes; don't lose her relationship with Him in the busyness of it.

Just because some verses are quoted often, we don't have to let them lose their power. One of them is in James two. It talks about how faith without works is dead. If I say I have faith yet let everyone else in the church do all the serving, while I just sit back and enjoy being served, what good is my faith. Who is it helping? Me? No, sadly, not even me. Colossians 3:23 *And whatever you do, do it heartily, as to the Lord and not to men.* If I do everything as if I am doing it for our Lord, then I wouldn't even have to say I have faith, the people around me would just know. James 2:18 *But someone will say, "You have faith, and I have works." Show me your faith without your works, and I will show you my faith by my works.*

I have to point out now, that after all this, and praising God for giving me the heart to tell Him "yes" when he rebuked me, life in the Pearson household has not been all that peachy. Has this surprised me? No, not even a little bit, because I know my enemy. I had a major victory, and I knew he wouldn't just stand idly by, saying, "oh well, I didn't win this one, maybe next time". No, my enemy was furious that his deception didn't continue in my life, he can't take it out on God, so he comes after me and those I love. Tim and I had been on the verge of fighting until I realized what was happening, told Tim about it and we laughed and said, well, no more. Guys, continue to pray for me, I don't mind airing all of my faults, as you can tell, I think y'all now know me pretty well, warts and all. Hopefully, this will just get more people to praying for this fellow sinner.

Chapter 12

Do You Truly Want Wisdom Over Riches?

For the past couple of days I have been crying out to God for our loved ones that are lost, for our youths that are falling for the evil ones lies and for the ones that are just sitting there, doing nothing. In Zephaniah one, God says He will stretch out His hand to many wicked people and things, including those who have turned back from following the Lord and not sought him, nor inquired of Him. In verse twelve the Lord says . . . *"I will search Jerusalem with lamps, and punish the men who are settled in complacency, who say in their hearts, 'The Lord will not do good, nor will He do evil.'"* Friends, my heart melted when I read those words. There are so many people that I know and love that fall into those two categories, those that have turned back and the complacent ones.

I told God, we, (my church family), have prayed, fasted and done all we know to do to encourage them to come back or get to know our Savior. I asked Him, "What now, Lord? What are we doing wrong?" The answer I got kind of shocked me. My Father brought to mind the story of Solomon, how when given a choice, he chose wisdom instead of riches to lead and guide God's people. I said, "But Lord, you know we want wisdom, not riches . . ." The Lord cut me off mid-cry and brought to mind the struggle I had last week of thinking how I was putting God first and how easily I was deceived into pushing my beautiful Savior out of first place and let busyness take first seat in my life. Some may wonder what that has to do with bringing people to, or back to, the Lord. Well, if God isn't first in our life, we won't be telling Him yes when He tells us to do something or maybe not even seeing the needs that God wants us to see, just the ones that affect us and our family. If God isn't first in our life, if we value *anything* over Him, we may not even hear His beautiful voice when He tries to speak to us.

Fellow warriors, ask God to search your hearts, don't be deceived as I was. These beautiful souls are worth having our hearts ripped with sorrow at the knowledge that riches (or anything else) are loved above wisdom in our life. Do as Solomon did, ask for wisdom on how to talk, act, or whatever it is God wants you to do to bring in the harvest during these end times. If wanting riches are hidden in your heart, just ask the Perfect Physician for a heart repair. Remember, He loves when we humble ourselves and ask for help!

My friends, if you think you are immune to the sins of pride and wanting riches, take a look at Hezekiah's life. He followed the Lord with all of his heart, he removed all the idols in the land, and he led the people in such a way that they followed the Lord in one accord. The Word says in 2 Kings 18:5 *He trusted in the Lord God of Israel, so that after him was none like him among all the kings of Judah, nor who were before him.* This king loved God, we know this because he was obedient.

The King of Assyria was attacking all the nations, Hezekiah allowed fear in his heart, and therefore, he formed an alliance with Egypt. God had told him not to do this; we are not to be unevenly yoked. My friends don't fall for the lie and allow fear into your heart. Fear will make you do many things you wouldn't normally do. You may be thinking, "Lisa, you can't control emotions!" True, you can't, but you can control who you allow to steer that emotion.

A few months ago I was plagued by fear. I am not scared of things, guys, really, I'm not. That is just not part of my personality. Now, I do have my few things from childhood, snakes, rats and heights. That's about it though. My husband was in Africa at this time, so, I guess that is why the evil one pounced so hard. Satan had me jumping at my own shadow, worried, did I lock the door, did I set the alarm, is this person mad at me, did I offend this person, are my parents okay, will someone hurt them, do they have all they need, what about Madison, is she okay . . . and the list just goes on and on about the things I was scared and worried over. A wonderful friend of mine at church, Sylvia, was pretty stern with me and called me down. She fussed at me for allowing satan to pull this trick on me. Guys, this fear had changed my whole personality. She said, "**Enough!** Now let's pray!" She prayed with me for this plague to be over. Anyway, a couple of nights later I was asleep and I woke up and saw something at the end of my bed, it looked like a tall dark figure. I kicked at it, then, I was just so tired of the fight, I said out loud, "ah, Jesus will take care of it." I rolled over and immediately went back to sleep.

Now, did I really see something? I don't know nor does it matter, the point was made. Deep in me, due to my foundation, I knew the Lord would take care of everything. I wouldn't allow my mind to be attacked anymore. The fear was gone. Every time satan tries to come at me with fear now, I just laugh and call for my Big Brother, Jesus, to come take care of the bully. Friends, don't allow satan to come in and take over your mind with fear, worry or whatever your weak spot is.

King Hezekiah allowed fear in and it changed him, changed what he would normally do. Because of this fear, studies showed that forty six of Judah's cities were destroyed and a little over two hundred thousand people were captured. Friends, when you allow fear in, or any sin for that matter, it doesn't just affect you, it affects all the people around you. Hezekiah gave Sennacherib a huge tribute, and, several of Hezekiah's daughters were taken as concubines. How sad is that, but, how often do we pay tribute to satan only to have our loved ones turned over to him? Do you give tribute by not being obedient to God, by not turning off the TV when something is on that sears your spirit, by listening to music that doesn't lift your spirit but depresses it, by putting making money before worshipping God, (I'm not talking about the people who have to work during worship service, I'm talking about the ones that work when it's not required so they can make more), or do you pay tribute by allowing pride in your life, over your house, cars, looks, etc . . . Only you know what is in your life that is "tribute" to satan. Now, ask God to show it to you and then ask Him how it is affecting those around you, I guarantee it is.

After this, Sennacherib sent the Tartan, with a great army, up against Hezekiah. He was cursing God, telling the people that God could not save them nor could Hezekiah save them. People, make no mistake, when you give tribute to the evil one, it will never be enough! He will come against you and bring war. When he comes against you, he will whisper in your ear horrible lies against our Holy God. Have you heard one of these, "God can't save you!" or "God doesn't love you or He wouldn't have allowed this to happen to you?" The one that I feel is the most often used lie is "God doesn't hear you and will never hear you because you sinned! You are scum and dirty and God is holy! You can't go to Him like this!" Children of God, don't fall for it, it is written, *for all have sinned and fall short of the glory of God.* Romans 3:23 If you fall for the lies or pay tribute, do not compound it by **not** going to Jehovah Ezer (The Lord our Helper.)

Finally, Hezekiah said, "**enough**", he quit allowing fear to rule him and went to God. He called for Isaiah the prophet. God assured Hezekiah that He had heard all the blasphemous words and He would take care of things. After this God allowed Hezekiah to prosper and God exalted him.

Hezekiah went through all of this and the end was the most pitiful thing I have ever heard. The king was near death and he cried out to the Lord. The Lord extended Hezekiah's life fifteen years. 2 Chronicles 32:25 *But Hezekiah did not repay according to the favor shown him, for his heart was lifted up; therefore wrath was looming over him and over Judah and Jerusalem.* Hezekiah showed the ambassadors of Babylon all his treasures; there was nothing in his kingdom that they did not see. God pronounced judgment on Hezekiah; He said that Babylon will take away Hezekiah's sons to be eunuchs in their land. I'm sure God's heart broke at Hezekiah's response. 2 Kings 20:19 *So Hezekiah said to Isaiah, "The word of the Lord which you have spoken is good!" For he said, "Will there not be peace and truth at least in my days?"*

No, my fellow Christians, don't be deceived into thinking pride and riches wouldn't affect you. I'm sure Hezekiah didn't think it would affect him either.

Conclusion

My fellow warriors, you have learned about many of my faults while reading this. I don't mind, I am truly hoping that me sharing them with you will make your life a bit easier. If not, maybe it will help you to not be deceived any longer. I know how our enemy wants to make you believe that you are the only one sinning, that all other Christians are perfect; as you can see, that is very much not true. The sad part is, my friend, I only put a few of my faults in here, there are so many more.

My main objective in writing this was to help people grow in Christ and to not give up. I am so tired of seeing people I love so much being deceived. Let's help each other to grow, keep fighting the fight and stay in the race. I can see the finish line and my Savior is right there cheering me on. My friend, it is so worth staying in the race, look Who's arms you get run into for the victory dance; The One who loved us when we were the most unlovable.

If you have any questions for me, please, find me on Facebook and inbox me. You can find me under Lisa Norred-Pearson.